Let's
PLAYGROUND

E.C. EMLEN SCHOOL
CHEW & UPSAL STS.
PHILADELPHIA, PA. 19119

BY EDWARD MYERS

Modern Curriculum Press

299 Jefferson Road, P.O. Box 480
Parsippany, NJ 07054 - 0480

Internet address:
http://www.pearsonlearning.com

Credits

Photos: 6—7: William Albert Allard/National Geographic Society. 8: Tyler Campbell. 13, 14, 15: Courtesy of Leathers & Associates. 17: Tyler Campbell. 20: Silver Burdett Ginn. 21: PhotoDisc, Inc. 23: ©Tim Davis/Photo Researchers, Inc. 25, 26, 27: Tyler Campbell. 28, 29: J.M. Mejuto. 30: Robert J. Bennett. 31: Jim Allor. 32, 33, 34, 35: Tyler Campbell. 36: J.M. Mejuto. 37, 38, 39: Tyler Campbell. 40: *l.* Courtesy of Leathers & Associates. 40—41: Tyler Campbell. 41: *t.,b.* Courtesy of Leathers & Associates. 42—43, 47: Tyler Campbell.

Design by Liz Kril

ISBN: 0-7652-0882-2

3 4 5 6 7 8 9 10 MA 05 04 03 02 01 00

Contents

Many thanks to Kelly Hayes and to her colleagues at Robert Leathers & Associates of Ithaca, New York, whose help was invaluable in creating this book.

Chapter 1

LET'S BUILD A PLAYGROUND!

"There's no place to play!" Many children say those words. There may be only an empty lot, a small field, or a concrete square where children can play games and bounce balls. If there is a playground in a park or a schoolyard, it may have just a slide and a couple of swings. In some places, there really is no place to play.

Many children have nowhere to play.

So the kids and the parents in a community decide it's time for a new playground. But a new playground costs a lot of money. Even a small one might cost $25,000. A really big playground might cost almost half a million dollars. How can a town afford such a costly project? They can do it if they make the playground a community project and build it themselves.

In the past, Americans often used to work this way. Farmers would help to build a neighbor's barn or harvest another family's crops. Americans are still willing to help each other when disaster strikes, such as a hurricane or a tornado. But community projects aren't as common as they used to be.

Traditional barn raising

When a community decides it wants a new playground, it must first answer some important questions.

- Where will we build the playground?
- What kind of a playground do we want?
- How do we build it?

A community parade for a playground project

Lots of people are needed to help plan and organize. Money must be collected, too, to pay for the playground. Many more people are needed to help with the building.

Building a playground is not an easy job. But many communities have done it. Let's find out how one community built a playground.

FUN FACTS

In 1990 a group of people from all over the country formed the Community Built Association. They wanted to help communities start their own building projects in which everyone works together.

Chapter 2

DESIGN DAY

After a place is chosen for the playground, a design comes next. When you design something, you decide what it looks like and how it works. Who will design this playground? The kids who will use it, of course! When it comes to playgrounds, kids are the experts.

A Design Day is set. On that day, a playground designer meets with the kids to help them plan the new playground. The designer is an architect. An architect is someone who knows how to design houses, buildings, and other places where people live, work, and play.

Children share playground ideas.

Kids' ideas for a playground

Every child who comes to the Design Day meeting will get a chance to say what he or she wants in the playground. If possible, every idea will become part of the playground.

The kids have thought up all sorts of great ideas for the playground. Many children want slides, swings, and bridges. Others ask for stairs, tunnels, ladders, rings, and sliding poles.

Some kids have special ideas. One child wants a tightrope. Another child wants a treehouse. Another wants a castle with tall towers, adding, "Connect the towers with a hanging walkway." Others suggest a clubhouse, a roller coaster, and a wooden dragon with a slide coming out of its mouth.

As the kids talk, the designer listens. She takes notes and makes sketches. Sometimes the kids give her drawings they have made of how they want the playground to look.

After she listens to the kids, the designer starts to work. She has a big piece of paper and some special pencils. While the kids watch, she starts to draw. The designer takes the kids' list of ideas and draws them one by one on the paper.

Children help the designer.

A designer's plan for a playground

Little by little, the design for the playground takes shape. The designer makes sure that all the different parts of the playground will fit together. The designer works for many hours. Sometimes, designing a playground takes all day!

Finally, the design is finished. Then, the designer meets with the children, their parents, grandparents, teachers, and the planning committee. She displays her design so that everyone can see it. She points out where she has put all the kids' ideas. The kids are excited when they see their ideas on paper. The playground is becoming more and more real!

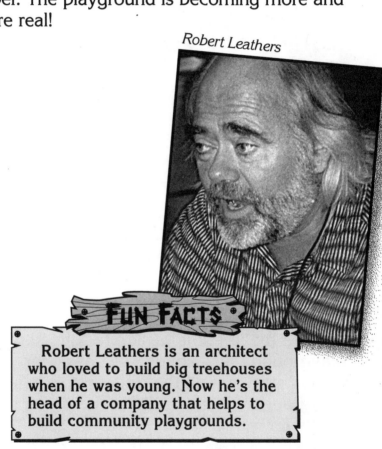

Robert Leathers

FUN FACTS

Robert Leathers is an architect who loved to build big treehouses when he was young. Now he's the head of a company that helps to build community playgrounds.

Chapter 3

Time to Get Ready

Now that the community has a design for a playground, it's time for the adults to get to work. All of the parents, grandparents, teachers, and other people who want to help have a lot to do.

Some of them help by joining committees. Committees are groups of people who work together to plan a job or to solve a problem. Members of a committee meet to talk about what needs to be done. Many committees are needed for the playground project. One of the most important is a committee to sign up volunteers, or people who agree to work on the playground for free.

Volunteers learn about the playground.

15

The materials committee works to find and buy materials. They call or visit local companies that sell construction supplies. They have to get boards, cement, nails, screws, paint, sandpaper, and other things. They ask the company owners to give some of the materials for free to help the playground project.

Another group gathers building tools. All kinds of tools are needed, from hammers and pliers to power saws. The group asks people to bring their tools. They also talk to companies who might donate tools.

The food committee members plan what they will feed all the workers on the days when the playground is being built. They may have to plan lunches and dinners for a hundred or more people for up to five days! That's a lot of food!

The child-care committee plans ways to look after younger children on the days when everyone will be busy building the playground. If the parents don't have child care, they might not be able to work on the project. So the committee thinks of all kinds of fun things the kids can do while their parents build.

Little by little, the adults plan everything that's needed to make the project possible.

FUN FACTS

In a community playground project, from 300 to 400 children may help do the work.

Chapter 4

KIDS GET READY, TOO!

What do the kids do while the adults are busy? They have lots of important jobs. They talk about the project to friends, neighbors, and family members. They make and put up signs to tell everyone about the playground project. They work with parents, teachers, and other adults to get ready for the hard work ahead.

Neighborhood signs ask for help.

One of the best ways the kids can help is to raise money. Because a playground is so expensive, people in the community have to figure out how to pay for the materials. The answer is fund-raising, which is doing all kinds of things to collect money.

There are many ways to raise funds. One idea is to hold a bake sale to sell bread, cakes, cookies, and pies. Some kids have a car wash. Then they give the money they earn to the playground project.

Kids wash cars to raise money.

A school fair and barbecue

Other kids set up a school fair. At a school fair, people pay money to play games, ride ponies, enter contests, and do other fun activities. There are many kinds of foods to buy, such as hot dogs, hamburgers, pizza, soda, and cotton candy. All of the money raised at the school activities goes to the playground project.

Choosing the winning ticket

The kids also plan a raffle, which is a contest to see who wins a prize. People buy tickets for a chance to win. The prize might be some toys, a fancy dinner, or even a bicycle. The money that is left over after paying for the prize will go to help pay for the playground.

On raffle day, one ticket is picked. The number on the ticket is read aloud. The person who bought that ticket wins the prize.

Another group of kids plans a jump-a-thon. In teams, they plan to take turns jumping rope for an hour and a half to raise money for the playground. Friends, family members, and neighbors agree to give the jumpers an amount of money for every minute they jump.

Jumping rope at a jump-a-thon

Another popular way to raise money is called "Pennies From Heaven." The kids collect extra pennies from their homes. They bring the pennies to school and put them in big plastic jugs. The money adds up quickly. Sometimes the kids bring enough pennies to cover the school gym floor! Schools have raised thousands of dollars this way.

It takes a long time to raise a lot of money. Without the kids, there would not be enough money, and the playground project would not be possible.

FUN FACTS

For a playground project in Fayetteville, Georgia, children raised over $10,000 in their penny drive.

Chapter 5

HOW MANY BOARDS
MAKE A PLAYGROUND?

The playground design is finished.
Everyone is working on raising money.
What's next?

After the designer finishes the playground
design, she figures out what materials will be
needed for such a big project. Building even a
small playground
requires a large
amount of
materials.

Some of these
materials are what
you would expect,
such as boards,
poles and stakes,
beams, long and
short nails, and
screws.

Boards for the playground

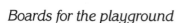

Other materials include clean play sand, concrete, pieces of stone, metal pipes, and lengths of chain. Playground projects also use sandpaper, glue, paint, tape, string, rope, and rubber hoses.

Some materials are ordinary things that might not seem to belong in a playground. How about tires? Some of the best materials for a modern playground are recycled truck and car tires. Tires can be used to make tunnels, towers, and swings.

These tires will become a part of a playground.

A power sander is used to make boards smooth.

Many kinds of big and small tools are also needed to build a playground. Some of the tools are power tools. Others are hand tools. Some of the workers will also use heavy equipment or big machines.

Many power tools are electric. Others run on gasoline. Some of these machines are chain saws, rotary saws, drills, sanders, and nail guns. The work goes much faster with these tools than it would without them.

One of the big machines the workers use is called a boom auger. A boom auger is used to drill deep, narrow holes. After the holes are drilled, the workers place wooden poles into the holes. The playground will be built around and on these poles.

A boom auger drills a hole for a wooden pole.

Big machines dig up the ground.

The workers also need a machine called a backhoe. The backhoe is a powerful machine used to dig holes and trenches.

The workers also need hand tools such as measuring tapes, hammers, saws, screwdrivers, and shovels. Some people will bring their own tools from home. Other tools are donated by building companies.

A volunteer sands boards.

Safety is important, too. Anyone who works with tools must wear safety glasses. The people who operate the big machines must know how to operate them.

All of the planning, the collecting of tools, and the signing up of workers may take months. It might seem as though the playground will never be built!

FUN FACTS

Most playground projects use two boom augers. The machines can dig about 200 holes in four to six hours. It would take 50 people more than two days to dig 200 holes with shovels.

Chapter 6

CONSTRUCTION BEGINS

The day finally arrives. It's time to start building the playground! Hundreds of adults and children show up at the site early in the morning.

It may be hard to believe, but a crew of volunteers can build even a large playground in only four or five days. The work goes fast when many people in a community work together.

Volunteers pick up tools and materials.

TOOLS/MATERIALS

To be part of the project, children sometimes take two or three days off from school. The time off isn't a vacation. It's hard work, and the children learn how to work as a team and help each other. But most kids are excited and want to help.

Work starts at seven in the morning and goes on all day. Many people will be at the construction site long after the sun goes down. Lights are set up so that people can keep working.

The playground site before building

Day 1 of the playground project

On the first day, adults work on the beginning stages of construction. One of the first steps is to dig holes with the boom auger. A pole is then set into each hole.

The poles look like telephone poles. Stuck deep in the ground, they are like the skeleton of the playground. They will support the walls, walkways, tunnels, towers, and other parts of the playground.

While the adults are busy sawing and hammering, kids are busy, too. Some of the jobs are for younger children. They help to specially prepare some of the materials before they can be used in the playground.

Some children scrub recycled tires, which makes the tires clean enough to be part of the playground.

Children scrub tires.

This girl sands a board.

Other kids sand boards with sandpaper. Boards are often rough. Sanding the boards makes them smooth and safe for the children who will be using the playground.

Another job for kids is coating screws with soap. Why would anyone coat screws with soap? The reason is that soap makes the screws much easier to put into the boards. This job may seem small, but it's important.

Children soap screws.

Other children paint pictures on boards. These boards will become part of the walls of the clubhouse.

Older children from 10 to 17 years old do other jobs. Some help the adults carry materials and tools. Others pound nails into boards.

Putting up boards

Sanding boards

College students do the same work as adults. Some of them saw boards. Others help build wooden floors, decks, and towers. Still others put up swings and other pieces of playground equipment.

Day 2 of the playground project

By the second day the playground starts to take shape. Now it's much more than a skeleton. There are walkways and towers. The supports for swings and other pieces of equipment are in place. It starts to look more like a playground.

FUN FACTS

For one playground project, about 3,600 people showed up to help. In just five days, they built a playground big enough for 550 children.

Chapter 7

A Playground at Last!

After three days, everyone is tired. Most of the volunteers aren't trained to do this kind of work. No one has rested much during the last few days. People are beginning to complain about sore muscles. It's already Friday and the work seems endless. But the playground is starting to look like a real playground.

The start of Day 4

The walkways have floors. The swing sets have frames.

There's a tightrope, a spider web, and a pirate ship.

There's a big castle, too, with turrets and towers. The castle even has a secret staircase that goes up to the towers.

There are two flat slides and a curved tunnel slide.

There's even a clubhouse.

Volunteers work at night to finish the playground.

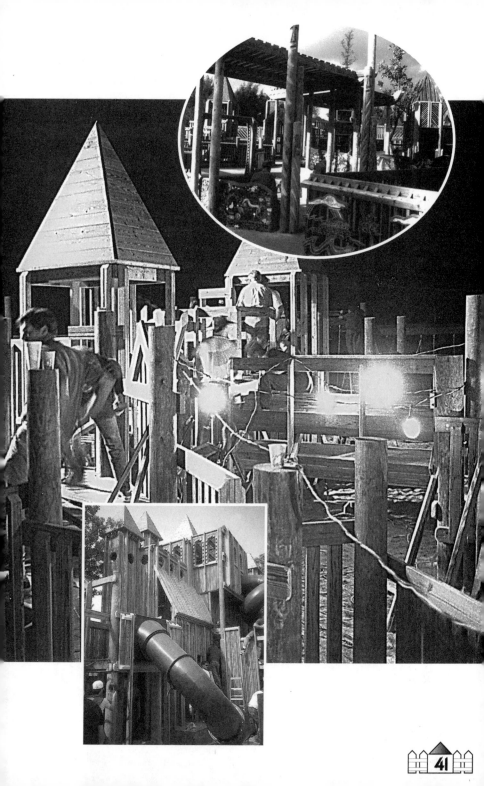

It's late Sunday afternoon now, the last day of the project. Almost all of the remaining pieces of equipment are in place. Children work hard at doing the final sanding so that all the surfaces are smooth.

Construction site on Day 5

Everyone at the site can see how close they are to finishing the playground. No one can believe what they see. The playground is much bigger than anyone had imagined.

Children get ready for the playground to open.

As the work comes to an end, all the volunteers leave the playground. They will be coming back soon, though. The adults and children will be getting ready for a special opening celebration.

On opening day, the kids wait eagerly near the entrance to the new playground they helped to create. Ribbons are stretched around the playground. Some people shout a countdown: "Ten! Nine! Eight! Seven! Six! ..."

When everyone shouts "Zero," the kids run forward. The ribbons break. The playground is open.

Some children race to spots they picked out ahead of time. Others don't know where to start. There are so many fun things to do.

Racing to the new playground

A place to play at last!

All the kids can now play in their new playground. And everyone—adults and children alike—feels proud about what they've been able to do by working so hard together.

Community volunteers are proud of their new playground.

FUN FACTS

Leathers & Associates have built thousands of playgrounds in the United States, Canada, Australia, and Israel. Each playground is different.

GLOSSARY

cement (suh MENT) a lime and clay powder that can be mixed with water to make a thick substance that hardens like stone when dry

committee (kuh MIHT ee) a small group of people who work together on something

community (kuh MYOO nuh tee) a group of people living in a town or a city

concrete (KAHN kreet) a hard substance made of cement, gravel, sand, and water that is used in buildings and sidewalks

construction (kun STRUK shun) something that is being built

donate (DOH nayt) to give something, such as money or materials, to help someone

project (PRAH jekt) a plan that takes much thinking and working together

recycle (ree SYE kul) to use something over again

site (syt) a place chosen for a building or an event

volunteer (vahl un TEER) someone who offers to work for free